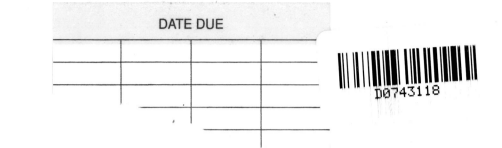

Sharon Sharth

Sharks and Rays

Underwater Predators

Dedicated to my shark, Mark
With special thanks to Gregor M. Cailliet, Professor, Moss Landing
Marine Laboratories

Photographs ©: Innerspace Visions: 23 (Gary Bell), 5 top right (Mark Conlin), 17 (C. & M. Fallows/Seapics.com), 5 top left, 33, (Howard Hall/Seapics.com), 42 (Doug Perrine), 5 bottom left, 13 (Doug Perrine/Seapics.com), 27 (Mark Strickland), 15, 41 (Ron & Valerie Taylor), 7, 37 (Masa Ushioda); Marine Mammal Images/Tershy & Strong: 31; Peter Arnold Inc.: 21, 24, 25 (Bob Evans), 38, 39 (Gerard Soury); Photo Researchers, NY: 1 (David Hall), 35 (A.B. Joyce), 43 (Fred McConnaughey), 5 bottom right, 6 (Tom McHugh/Steinhart Aquarium), 40 (Sinclair Stammers/SPL); Stone: 19 (Martin Barraud), cover (Jeff Rotman), 29 (Stuart Westmorland).

Illustrations by Pedro Julio Gonzalez, Steve Savage and A. Natacha Pimentel C.

The photo on the cover shows a great white shark. The photo on the title page shows a blue-spotted stingray.

Library of Congress Cataloging-in-Publication Data

Sharth, Sharon.
    Sharks and rays: underwater predators / Sharon Sharth; [Pedro Julio Gonzalez
and A. Natacha Pimentel, illustrators].
      p. cm. — (Animals in order)
    Includes bibliographical references and index.
    ISBN 0-531-11868-1
1. Sharks—Juvenile literature. 2. Rays (Fishes)—Juvenile literature. [1. Sharks. 2. Rays (Fishes)]
I. Gonzalez, Pedro Julio, ill. II. Pimentel, A. Natacha, ill. III. Title. IV. Series.

QL638.9 .S52 2001

2001017957

Contents

Is That a Shark or a Ray?

Are you afraid of sharks and rays? Do their sharp teeth and pointy barbs fill you with dread? All sharks and rays are meat-eaters, and these *predators* eat almost every kind of animal that lives in the ocean. Do you think that these fierce creatures couldn't possibly be related to anything you know? Think again! Sharks and rays are fishes. Like other fishes, they live underwater and obtain oxygen by breathing through *gills*.

Most fishes are *cold blooded*. This means that their body temperatures match their surroundings and change as their surroundings change. You are *warm blooded*. Your temperature stays close to 98.6 degrees Fahrenheit (37 degrees Celsius) no matter what the temperature is outside your body.

Sharks and rays have many traits that are different from other fishes. All four of the animals shown on the next page are fishes. Only three of them are a shark or a ray. Can you tell which one is *not* a shark or a ray?

Basking shark

Manta ray

Spotted wobbegong

Piranha

Traits of Sharks and Rays

Sharks and rays have rows of teeth.

Did you choose the piranha? Even with its daggerlike teeth, this fish is not a shark or a ray. Sharks and rays have skeletons made of flexible *cartilage* instead of hard bone. Cartilage is the same matter that makes up the tip of your nose and your ears. Sharks and rays have rows of teeth that are constantly replaced as old teeth fall out. Denticles, toothlike scales, cover their skin. Some denticles are soft while others feel like sandpaper. Some will even cut your hand!

Another way that sharks and rays differ from many other fishes is that sharks and rays don't have *swim bladders*. Swim bladders are organs inflated with gases that help fishes float. Sharks and rays need to stay in constant motion. If they don't swim, they sink to the ocean floor. However, some sharks can float with the help of their liver. The liver stores oil in the body. Since oil is lighter than water, a liver containing stored oil helps a shark to stay afloat.

Like you, sharks and rays have five senses—smell, sound, touch, sight, and taste. Plus, they have one more. They can sense electrical fields. All animals give off electricity controlled by their heart rates, respiration, and muscle movements. Sharks and rays have a greater sensitivity to these currents than any other animal. This sensitivity contributes to their ability to hunt well.

How can you tell the difference between sharks and rays? Most sharks have long, slender bodies. Rays are more circular and flat. Some rays have the largest *pectoral fins* of any fishes. They extend all along the sides of their bodies. Rays swim by fluttering these fins. The pectoral fins on the side of a shark are used to lift the shark in the water. These fins are also used to stop the shark from moving forward—like brakes. A ray's gill openings are under its head. A shark's gill openings are in front of its pectoral fins on either side of its body.

A shark swims by sweeping its *caudal fin* from side to side. The fin is usually longer on the top, which gives the shark extra speed. Most ray tails are narrow and are used for balance or steering.

Rays have no *dorsal fin*. The dorsal fin on a shark's back keeps it from rolling over. This is the fin you see sticking up out of the water just before someone yells, "Shark!"

Can you see this manta ray's gills?

The Order of Living Things

A tiger has more in common with a house cat than with a daisy. A true bug is more like a butterfly than a jellyfish. Scientists arrange living things into groups based on how they look and how they act. A tiger and a house cat belong to the same group, but a daisy belongs to a different group.

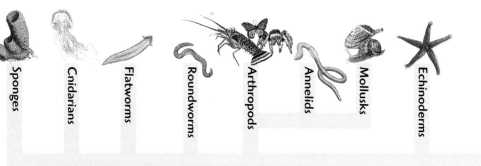

Sponges · Cnidarians · Flatworms · Roundworms · Arthropods · Annelids · Mollusks · Echinoderms

Animals

Plants · Fungi

Protists

Monerans

All living things belong to one of five groups called *kingdoms*: the plant kingdom, the animal kingdom, the fungus kingdom, the moneran kingdom, or the protist kingdom. You can probably name many of the creatures in the plant and animal kingdoms. The fungus kingdom includes mushrooms, yeasts, and molds. The moneran and protist kingdoms contain thousands of living things that are too small to see without a microscope.

8

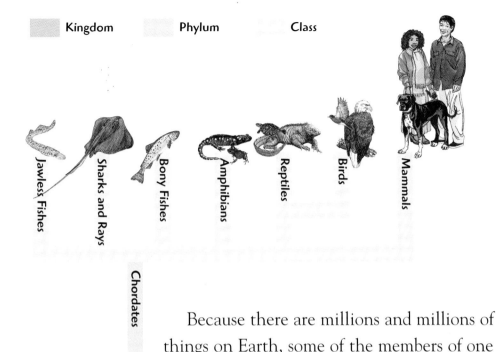

Kingdom   Phylum   Class

Jawless Fishes

Sharks and Rays

Bony Fishes

Amphibians

Reptiles

Birds

Mammals

Chordates

Because there are millions and millions of living things on Earth, some of the members of one kingdom may not seem all that similar. The animal kingdom includes creatures as different as tarantulas and trout, jellyfish and jaguars, salamanders and sparrows, elephants and earthworms.

To show that an elephant is more like a jaguar than an earthworm, scientists further separate the creatures in each kingdom into more specific groups. The animal kingdom is divided into nine *phyla*. Humans belong to the chordate phylum. All chordates have a backbone.

Each phylum can be subdivided into many *classes*. Humans, mice, and elephants all belong to the mammal class. Each class is divided into *orders*; orders are divided into *families*, families into *genera*, and genera into *species*. All the members of a species are very similar and can mate and produce healthy young.

9

How Sharks and Rays Fit In

You can probably guess that sharks and rays belong to the animal kingdom. They have much more in common with swordfish and snakes than with maple trees and morning glories.

Sharks and rays belong to the chordate phylum. Almost all chordates have a backbone and a skeleton. Can you think of other chordates? Examples include elephants, mice, snakes, birds, and whales.

The chordate phylum can be divided into a number of classes. Sharks and rays belong to the chondrichthyes (kon-DRIK-thees) class. Chondrichthyes means "cartilaginous fishes" and refers to the cartilage that makes up their skeletons.

Sharks and rays are part of the subclass elasmobranchii. Elasmobranchs are divided into two different orders—selachii for sharks and batoidea for rays. Orders are divided into a number of different families and genera. These groups can be broken down into hundreds of species. In this book, you will learn more about fourteen different species of sharks and rays.

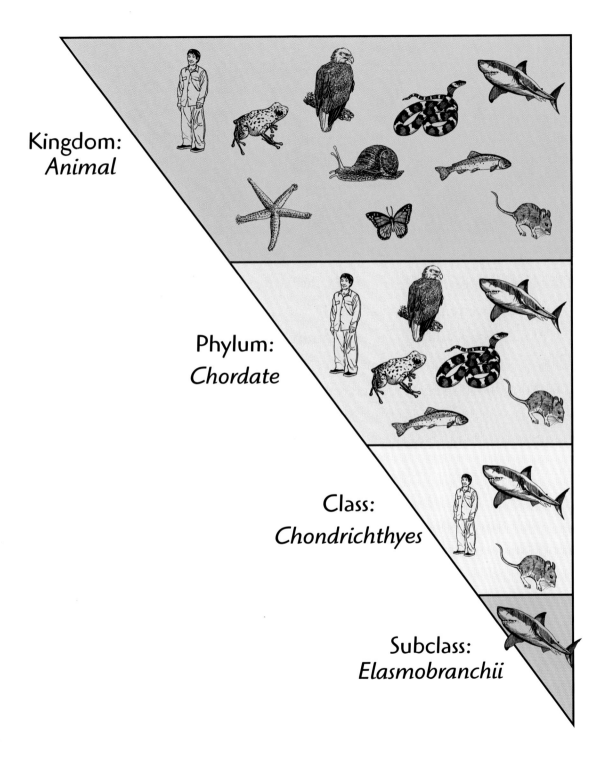

Kingdom:
Animal

Phylum:
Chordate

Class:
Chondrichthyes

Subclass:
Elasmobranchii

11

Gray Sharks

FAMILY: Carcharhinidae
COMMON EXAMPLE: Tiger shark
GENUS AND SPECIES: *Galeocerdo cuvieri*
SIZE: 10 to 18 feet (3 to 5.5 m)

A lone tiger shark prowls the tropical coastal waters in search of *prey*. One of the most dangerous sharks, it can swim 50 miles (80 km) a day. It stops only to eat.

Weighing in at about 2,200 pounds (999 kg), a tiger shark gets its name from the dark lines on its back. The lines look like tiger stripes. They fade as the shark ages. Tiger sharks may live as long as 30 or 40 years.

No animal that lives in the coral reef is safe from the tiger shark—it will eat practically everything in its path. It will pounce on sea lions and grab gulls from the surface of the water. Known as the "garbage can shark," it will devour other fishes, sea turtles, seabirds, shoes, license plates, raincoats, and people. But humans are not a regular part of any shark's diet. It's not unusual for a shark to take a bite of a person, dislike like the taste, and spit it out.

There are between 30 and 50 reported shark attacks against humans each year throughout the world. Few of these are fatal. In fact, you have a better chance of getting hit by lightning than you do of being attacked by a shark!

Hammerhead Sharks

FAMILY: *Sphyrnidae*
COMMON EXAMPLE: Great hammerhead shark
GENUS AND SPECIES: *Sphyrna mokarran*
SIZE: 2 to 20 feet (60 cm to 6 m)

The great hammerhead shark swings its wide, flat head back and forth as it surveys the ocean floor. It's looking for its next meal of stingrays or some other prey. This odd-looking shark has one eye and one nostril on either end of its T-shaped head. These organs are separated for a reason. Having an eye on each side gives the shark better vision. A nostril on both ends adds to the hammerhead's excellent sense of smell.

These sharks live in tropical waters. They can also be found in warm *temperate* waters. Many sharks eat other sharks, and the hammerhead is no exception. A 9-foot (3-m)-long lemon shark was once found in the stomach of a 15-foot (5-m)-long hammerhead shark!

Great hammerhead sharks give birth the same way that mammals do. The baby develops inside its mother. Food and oxygen is transferred from the mother to the baby shark through an organ that is like an umbilical cord. When the pup is born, it breaks the cord by quickly swimming away before its mother has a chance to eat it.

14

15

Mackerel Sharks

FAMILY: Lamnidae
COMMON EXAMPLE: Great white shark
GENUS AND SPECIES: *Carcharodon carcharias*
SIZE: 19.5 feet (6 m)

The great white shark smells blood. It spies an injured sea lion. With a twitch of its tail fin, the shark torpedoes toward its prey. It surprises and attacks the sea lion by coming at it from behind and below. Just before the shark takes its first bite, it lifts its head out of the water to unhinge its huge lower jaw. Then its eyes roll back into its head to protect them from damage while feeding. The shark's teeth cut into the sea lion and tear it apart.

The great white has the largest teeth of any shark! They are 3 inches (8 cm) long, triangular, sharp, and jagged. Add those teeth to the great white's hunting ability and speed, and you'll understand why this shark is one of the most respected creatures in the ocean.

These sharks don't chew their food. After the first bite, they let the prey bleed to death. Then they tear it into chunks and swallow the pieces whole. Great whites travel in the upper layers of tropical and temperate waters. They prefer to eat sea lions and seal pups, but they will also dine on swordfish and other sharks.

The great white shark rivals the tiger shark in its attacks on humans. A surfer may look like a seal or a sea lion to this shark.

Stingrays
FAMILY: Dasyatidae
COMMON EXAMPLE: Common stingray
GENUS AND SPECIES: *Dasyatis pastinaca*
SIZE: 8 feet (2.5 m)

With its flat, wide body and long, thin tail, the stingray moves slowly along the ocean floor. Covered with mud or sand, it remains hidden from its enemies and its prey. It mainly feeds on mollusks such as snails and clams. The stingray's flat, hard teeth and powerful jaws are ideal for cracking their shells open.

Stingrays are shy creatures. Many live in warm, shallow sections of tropical oceans or temperate seas. Some even live in freshwater. Their smooth skin is dark green or black.

Be careful not to step on a stingray at the beach! When threatened, its whiplike tail will swing up and stick a venomous spine deep into the flesh of its enemy. The venom is produced from glands along the sides of the spine. The stingray's wound affects the victim's heart and nervous system, and it causes paralysis and nausea. Although it is very painful, it is rarely fatal to humans.

It's a good idea to shuffle your feet when you wade in shallow waters where stingrays live. This will let them know you're coming. If a stingray has any kind of warning, it will swim away rather than sting you.

18

19

Electric Rays

FAMILY: Torpedinidae
COMMON EXAMPLE: Pacific electric ray
GENUS AND SPECIES: *Torpedo californica*
SIZE: 6 inches to 7 feet (15 cm to 2.1 m)

Although many electric ray species live in warm, shallow coastal waters, some are found 1,200 feet (366 m) below the surface! These rays often lie buried in sand on the bottom of the sea. Their tiny eyes are the only part of their bodies that betray their location.

These rays stay very still during the day. At night, they swim through rocky reefs hunting for worms, small fishes, shellfish, and other crustaceans. Most electric rays are dark brown, blue, or gray with spots. They have long, thin, pointy tails with fins. A female electric ray gives birth to live young. Between 3 and 21 eggs hatch inside her body.

Electric rays move slowly, but they attack with gusto. They generate their own electricity to stun prey or ward off predators. On either side of the head are large organs that give off a 200-volt shock! The electrical outlets at your house give only 120 volts. After one good shock, however, the electric ray must recharge itself by resting.

Carpet Sharks

FAMILY: Orectolobidae
COMMON EXAMPLE: Spotted wobbegong
GENUS AND SPECIES: *Orectolobus maculatus*
SIZE: 8 feet (2.5 m)

The spotted wobbegong shark lies as still as a carpet covering the ocean floor. Partly buried in sand, its spotted, brownish skin blends into its surroundings. A tiny spine sticks up out of its mouth and wiggles in the water. An unsuspecting damselfish swims too close. It mistakes the spine for food. CHOMP! The wobbegong grabs the fish with its knifelike teeth and sucks it into its mouth.

These sharks don't go hunting—they wait for their prey to come to them. They feed at night on a diet of crabs, lobsters, octopuses, other invertebrates, and small fishes.

Wobbegong sharks are most often found in the shallow waters of tropical Australian seas. Their spotted or striped markings help to hide them against rocky landscapes and areas teeming with seaweed and eelgrass. Skin flaps on their heads also help them blend in with their surroundings. The flaps look like algae, a simple plantlike organism that usually lives in water. In front of each nostril, a pointy spine sticks out. Tendrils poke out from their jaws and make the wobbegong look as though it has a beard!

Horn Sharks

FAMILY: Heterodontidae
COMMON EXAMPLE: Horn shark
GENUS AND SPECIES: *Heterodontus francisci*
SIZE: 3 feet (1 m)

The horn shark is well-hidden from its underwater enemies in the temperate ocean waters. Its brown and pale yellow skin tones match the kelp forest vegetation where it hides in caves and under rocks during the day. It feeds only at night.

This shark is nicknamed the "pig shark" because of its piglike snout. A horn shark has a highly developed sense of smell. Like most sharks, it can smell a few drops of blood more than a mile away.

Horn sharks can also smell clams buried under the sand. They crawl across the ocean floor on their pectoral fins to get to the soft-shelled crabs and spiny urchins on which they feed. They easily break the shells apart using their strong, flat teeth. A sharp spine, which looks like a horn, sticks out from each dorsal fin.

The female horn shark releases her eggs in areas where they are sure to fall between rocks or in small crevices. Horn shark eggs are covered by screw-shaped cases that become trapped in tight places. The eggs are then protected from predators for the 6 to 9 months before they hatch.

Eagle Rays

FAMILY: *Myliobatidae*
COMMON EXAMPLE: Common eagle ray
GENUS AND SPECIES: *Aetobatus narinari*
SIZE: 10 feet (3 m)

Eagle rays are social animals that sometimes swim in groups, or schools. When they flap their pectoral fins, they look like a flock of birds in flight. Even their snouts look like bird beaks! Their flattened bodies and long, thin tails sail across the tropical or warm temperate seas just under the surface of the water. Eagle rays are also found in shallow lagoons, bays, and in coastal waters.

A glossy, greenish sheen covers the eagle ray's back. Shimmering in the sun, this sheen reflects off the water. The eagle ray's back may be covered with dots that range in color from white and yellow to green. The dots help the ray blend in with its surroundings and hide it from predators and prey.

The eagle ray dives to the sandy ocean floor in search of mussels, snails, crabs, and other crustaceans. Like the stingray, an eagle ray will use its flat, strong molarlike teeth to snap apart their shells.

Behind the dorsal fin at the base of the eagle ray's tail is a sharp, jagged spine. The ray uses this spine and its poisonous gland to protect itself from predators.

A new eagle ray hatches from an egg inside its mother. An adult female will birth 3 to 7 young at one time.

Whale Sharks

FAMILY: Rhincodontidae
COMMON EXAMPLE: Whale shark
GENUS AND SPECIES: *Rhincodon typus*
SIZE: 60 feet (18.3 m)

Whale sharks are the largest living fishes in the world. These polka-dotted sharks can weigh up to 20 tons (18,144 kg)! One whale shark is bigger than two African elephants and longer than a school bus.

Whale sharks are found in the warm, tropical regions of the Atlantic, Pacific, and Indian oceans. These gentle giants swim in herds just below the surface of the water. They feast on *plankton*, small fishes, squid, and shrimps.

Whale sharks have more than 300 rows of teeth in each jaw with hundreds of teeth in each row. But they don't use their surprisingly tiny, nubby teeth when they eat. They swim with their mouths wide open, and 250,000 gallons (946 l) of seawater per hour flows through their gills. The food is then filtered through a *gill raker*, a bristly comblike strainer, and swallowed.

The skin of a whale shark is like the rubber tires on trucks. Whale sharks have the thickest skin of any living animal. A 50-foot (15 m)-long whale shark has skin 6 inches (15 cm) thick. The trouble is, it's not strong enough to protect them from people. Whale sharks are often seriously injured or killed when rammed by ships.

Thresher Sharks

FAMILY: Alopiidae
COMMON EXAMPLE: Thresher shark
GENUS AND SPECIES: *Alopias vulpinus*
SIZE: 20 feet (6 m)

Threshers are found in both tropical and temperate seas. They are produced from eggs that hatch inside their mother's body. If the growing thresher pup uses up the yolk sac that nourishes it before birth, it will gorge on its mother's unfertilized eggs. Between 4 and 6 pups are born from each litter.

A thresher shark can jump completely out of the water when trying to catch prey or outswim a predator. It has a tail as long as, or even longer than, its body. Swimming at the surface of the ocean, the thresher shark uses its tail to gather together, or herd, schools of small fishes, such as sardines, anchovies, or mackerel. The tail becomes a whip that stuns or kills the fishes before the shark swallows them whole. This is how the thresher shark got its name. It threshes, or wildly strikes, its prey before it feeds.

Fishers sometimes catch threshers by their tails instead of by their mouths. This happens when a thresher whips its tail at the hook. Threshers have been overfished in recent years because of their light, tender meat. Their survival is a great concern to scientists, fishers, and conservationists.

31

Basking Sharks

FAMILY: Cetorhinidae
COMMON EXAMPLE: Basking shark
GENUS AND SPECIES: *Cetorhinus maximus*
SIZE: 46 feet (14 m)

The basking shark is the second largest shark after the whale shark. It is found in many of the world's oceans, especially in temperate waters. These shy creatures sometimes swim in schools of up to 250 animals. They get their name from the way they bask in the sun, or sunbathe, with their backs sticking out of the water. They may be enjoying the warmth of the sun, or they may be feeding on plankton.

Basking sharks, like whale sharks, open their huge mouths and take in the water and plankton as they swim along the surface of the ocean. They filter thousands of gallons of water per hour through their gill rakers. The plankton gets trapped by a sticky mucus that covers the gill rakers. Then the basking shark swallows the plankton. A basking shark needs to eat more than a half ton (454 kg) of plankton at every meal! Adult basking sharks weigh about 6 tons (5,443 kg).

Basking sharks may be gray, black, or brown. They give birth every other year to only 1 or 2 pups per litter. In the past, they have been overfished for the oil found in their large livers.

Spiny Dogfish Sharks

FAMILY: Squalidae
EXAMPLE: Spiny dogfish shark
GENUS AND SPECIES: *Squalus acanthias*
SIZE: 4 feet (1.21 m)

Spiny dogfish sharks are the most common and the most abundant sharks in our oceans. Found in temperate seas and in subarctic waters, these sharks are caught and used as food, fertilizer, and pet food by humans.

Female spiny dogfish sharks don't begin to reproduce until they are about 20 years old. It takes the 8 or more eggs almost 2 years to develop and hatch inside the mother. That's longer than the time it takes for an elephant to grow inside its mother! Spiny dogfish sharks may live to be more than 70 years old.

Hundreds of these small, gray sharks travel together in schools just above the ocean floor. Feeding in packs, they hunt squid, crabs, shrimps, and fishes. Spiny dogfish sharks are relentless as they pursue their prey, and they have been known to swim great distances in search of food. Using their sharp teeth, they will often steal easy prey by chewing through fishing nets.

These sharks get their name, spiny dogfish, from the spine that sticks out from each dorsal fin. They were also given this name because they hunt in packs the way dogs do.

Manta Rays

FAMILY: *Mobulidae*
COMMON EXAMPLE: Atlantic manta ray
GENUS AND SPECIES: *Manta birostris*
SIZE: 23 feet (7 m)

Manta rays are called "devil fish" because of the hornlike offshoots at the top of their heads. These are the largest rays. They may weigh up to 3,000 pounds (1,362 kg). That's as heavy as a small car!

A manta ray is dark brown or black on top and white underneath. It has a small tail, no stinging spine, and tiny teeth only in its lower jaw. These rays feed on small fishes, crustaceans, and plankton. They push the food into their wide mouths using the two arms, or horns, that are connected to their snouts. These horns are actually curled-up fins. Like the whale and basking sharks, manta rays filter food from the water using gill rakers.

Manta rays live in the upper waters of tropical open seas. They flap their huge pectoral fins like wings as they glide through the ocean. When their pectoral fins are spread open, manta rays have a wider wingspan than a small airplane! They can even leap high out of the water.

Female manta rays will often give birth while leaping. Only one live pup is born, usually once a year. A newborn manta ray weighs about 20 pounds (9 kg).

Sixgill Sharks

FAMILY: Hexanchidae
COMMON EXAMPLE: Bluntnose sixgill shark
GENUS AND SPECIES: *Hexanchus griseus*
SIZE: 16 feet (5 m)

The bottom layers of the ocean are dark and very cold. The water pressure builds as you go deeper. Food is scarce. Most fishes, including the bluntnose sixgill shark, move slowly and grow slowly at these depths.

The bluntnose sixgill shark is one of the most common and primitive creatures in the sea. It has six gills on each side of its body instead of the usual five pairs of most other sharks. This brown-colored predator rests on the seafloor most of the time, but it probably migrates upward at night to hunt. Sixgill sharks have been seen in the upper layers of the ocean and at 5,000 feet (1,525 m)! With their sharp, sawlike teeth, they eat large fishes— including other sharks and rays— crustaceans, and squid.

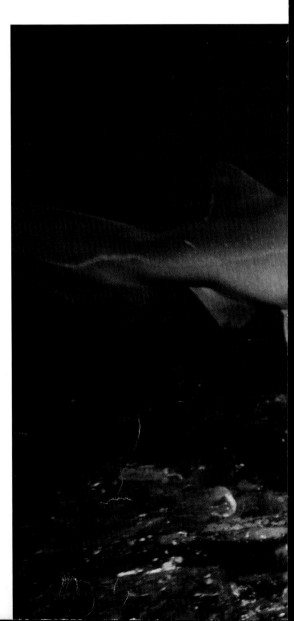

38

Like most sharks, the bluntnose sixgill shark is not dangerous to humans unless threatened. It is found all over the world in tropical and temperate seas, and it is fished for its meat and oil.

Bluntnose sixgill shark eggs hatch and develop inside their mother's body. These sharks may have more than 100 pups in each litter!

Saving Sharks and Rays

This fossil is the head of a Jurassic shark.

Sharks have roamed the world's oceans for more than 400 million years, even before the dinosaurs. Rays are descendants of sharks and have been around for 200 million years. But things are changing in the lives of these animals. Humans pose the greatest threat to their continued existence.

Sharks are not the ruthless killing machines we once believed them to be. They have actually killed under 300 people in the past hundred years! Many more people have died from bee stings and car crashes than from shark attacks. Many sharks strike only when threatened and would rather flee than fight. But most attacks are accidental. The shark mistakes the human for its usual prey. It takes a bite and swims away.

However, about 770,000 tons (700 million kg) of sharks and rays are killed every year by humans through recreational and commercial fishing. That equals more than 100 million sharks and rays!

This diver is killing a sand tiger shark.

Spiny dogfish sharks have recently been so overfished that their survival is threatened. The number of great white sharks is declining around the world even with laws in place to protect them in Australia, the southern tip of Africa, and parts of the United States. The two largest sharks, the whale and basking sharks, are also dropping in numbers. Scientists believe that the worldwide populations of some sharks have declined by 80 percent.

Sharks and rays can't breed as fast as they are being killed. Some give birth to only 2 pups every other year, so overfishing causes their numbers to drop dramatically. It takes years to reverse this kind of damage. It could eventually result in the extinction of entire species.

Many sharks are caught for sport during popular shark fishing competitions. Others drown when trapped in tuna nets or drifting squid nets. Unable to swim backward, they become hopelessly tangled. Longlines, fishing lines fitted with thousands of hooks, stretch across the ocean and accidentally trap sharks and rays. As the shark

These hammerhead sharks are caught in a fishing net.

or ray struggles to free itself, it becomes hooked and wrapped in the rope. If a shark or ray is unable to swim, the water doesn't flow across its gills, and it suffocates.

Many sharks are killed during finning, a practice in which the shark is caught and its fins are cut off. The shark is then thrown back into the sea where it bleeds to death. The fins are used to make shark fin soup that costs $100 a bowl. About 35 million pounds (16 million kg) of shark are discarded in this way each year.

Although sharks and rays seem to be immune to the pollution spreading through our oceans, their prey is not. If we destroy the food they eat, these creatures cannot survive. Sharks and rays help to regulate the health of our seas by freeing the waters of defective and diseased animals. Their existence ensures our own survival in the delicate balance of nature.

Dorsal fins of sharks dry in the sun.

Words to Know

cartilage—the strong, flexible matter which makes up the skeletons of sharks and rays

caudal fin—the tail fin of fishes

class—a group of creatures within a phylum that shares certain characteristics

cold blooded—having a body temperature that changes as air or water temperature changes

dorsal fin—the fin on the back of many aquatic animals

family—a group of creatures within an order that shares similar characteristics

genus (plural **genera**)—a group of creatures within a family that shares certain characteristics

gill—one of the body organs that remove oxygen from water and move it into a fish's blood

gill raker—a comblike device where plankton collects before being swallowed

kingdom—one of the five divisions into which all living things are placed: the animal kingdom, the plant kingdom, the fungus kingdom, the moneran kingdom, and the protist kingdom

order—a group of creatures that shares certain characteristics

pectoral fins—the fins that stick out from the sides of many fishes and other underwater animals

phylum (plural **phyla**)—a group of creatures within a kingdom that shares certain characteristics

plankton—a group of tiny floating plants and animals

predator—an animal that hunts and eats other animals

prey—an animal that is hunted and eaten by other animals

species—a group of creatures within a genus that shares certain characteristics. Members of the same species can mate and produce young.

swim bladder—an organ that is filled with gases and keeps certain fish from sinking

temperate—neither too hot nor too cold

warm blooded—having a body temperature that stays the same no matter how cold or warm it is outside

Learning More

Books

Arnold, Caroline. *Watch Out for Sharks!* New York: Clarion Books, 1994.

Berger, Melvin. *Chomp: A Book About Sharks.* New York: Scholastic, 1999.

Berman, Ruth. *Sharks.* Minneapolis, MN: Carolrhoda Books, 1995.

Markle, Sandra. *Outside and Inside Sharks.* New York: Atheneum Books for Young Readers, 1996.

Pipe, Jim. *The Giant Book of Sharks and Other Scary Predators.* Providence, RI: Copper Beech Books, 1999.

Rustad, Martha E. H. *Rays: Ocean Life.* Chicago: Pebble Books, 2001.

Simon, Seymour. *Sharks.* New York: HarperCollins, 1995.

Web Sites

Enchanted Learning
http://www.enchantedlearning.com/subjects/sharks
This site features fun illustrations and interesting facts about sharks and rays.

The Shark Foundation
http://www.shark.ch
This site supports the protection and preservation of endangered shark species and their natural surroundings.

Index

About the Author

Sharon Sharth is a certified scuba diver and has worked with dolphins at the Kewalo Basin Marine Mammal Laboratory in Hawaii. She has written many books about animals for children including *Jellyfish*, *Squid*, *Hawks*, *Robins*, *Finches*, *Rabbits*, and *Whales*. She has written a book about navigation, *Way to Go: Finding Your Way with a Compass*, and a book about time, *What Time Is It?* Ms. Sharth has been involved with children for many years as a teacher and as a Screen Actors Guild *Book Pal* reader. She believes that, through our children, the creatures with whom we share the Earth will finally come to be protected and respected.